The Inheritance of Haunting

THE ANDRÉS MONTOYA POETRY PRIZE

2004, *Pity the Drowned Horses*, Sheryl Luna
Final Judge: Robert Vasquez

2006, *The Outer Bands*, Gabriel Gomez
Final Judge: Valerie Martínez

2008, *My Kill Adore Him*, Paul Martínez Pompa
Final Judge: Martín Espada

2010, *Tropicalia*, Emma Trelles
Final Judge: Silvia Curbelo

2012, *A Tongue in the Mouth of the Dying*, Laurie Ann Guerrero
Final Judge: Francisco X. Alarcón

2014, *Furious Dusk*, David Campos
Final Judge: Rhina P. Espaillat

2016, *Of Form & Gather*, Felicia Zamora
Final Judge: Edwin Torres

2018, *The Inheritance of Haunting*, Heidi Andrea Restrepo Rhodes
Final Judge: Ada Limón

The Andrés Montoya Poetry Prize, named after the late California native and author of the award-winning book, *The Iceworker Sings*, supports the publication of a first book by a Latino or Latina poet. Awarded every other year, the prize is administered by Letras Latinas—the literary program of the Institute for Latino Studies at the University of Notre Dame.

heidi andrea restrepo rhodes

The Inheritance of Haunting

University of Notre Dame Press
Notre Dame, Indiana

Published by the University of Notre Dame Press
Notre Dame, Indiana 46556
undpress.nd.edu

Published in the United States of America

Library of Congress Cataloging-in-Publication Data

Names: Rhodes, Heidi Andrea, author.
Title: The inheritance of haunting / Heidi Andrea Restrepo Rhodes.
Description: Notre Dame, Indiana : University of Notre Dame Press, [2019] |
    Series: The Andres Montoya Poetry Prize | Includes bibliographical
    references. |
Identifiers: LCCN 2018055513 (print) | LCCN 2018059203 (ebook) | ISBN
    9780268105396 (pdf) | ISBN 9780268105402 (epub) | ISBN 9780268105372
    (hardback : alk. paper) | ISBN 0268105375 (hardback : alk. paper) | ISBN
    9780268105389 (pbk. : alk. paper) | ISBN 0268105383 (pbk. : alk. paper)
Classification: LCC PS3618.H626 (ebook) | LCC PS3618.H626 A6 2019 (print) |
    DDC 811/.6—dc23
LC record available at https://lccn.loc.gov/2018055513

∞ *This book is printed on acid-free paper.*

for my mamita, always

for the dead who keep close

for these glimmers, futures,
life otherwise, convulsive beauty,
the unruly mess alive, we
rake from the rubble & shadows

contents

II. CASI PÁJAROS/ALMOST BIRDS

acknowledgments

I offer my sincere thank you to the editors of the following publications in which versions of these poems first appeared:

Acentos Review: "the ache on the tongue of the grieving," "azan, or the call to prayer, o resistir es rezar que arrasemos el orden de arrancamiento, or when the sky opens & I am swallowed," and "little birds"

Adrienne: "the flower husband"

Colorism Healing (2014 Colorism Healing Poetry Contest, honorable mention): "all that is left"

Connotation Press: "the dream in which we die together"

Crabfat: "the heresy in our bones"

Decomp Magazine: "prayer for the children who will be born with today's daggers in their tomorrow eyes"

Feminist Studies Journal: "helix/womb/house"

Heavy Feather Review: "purgatory"

Kudzu House Review: "imbunche"

Library Blog (University of California, San Diego): "what the bird has seen"

Literature of War: At Home and Abroad (Scintilla Press, 2014): "noncombat related incidents & other lies"

Mixed Up! A Mixed Race Queer and Feminist Zine: "missionary"

Movement of Queer Diasporas, art exhibition, Multicultural Community Center, University of California, Berkeley, October 2012: "missionary"

Nepantla: A Journal for Queer Poets of Color: "the terror of clean"

Pank: "when the machete will sever the ballad (memory-mourning for El Mozote)"

Pariahs, ed. Sarah Rafael Garcia and mónica teresa ortiz (Stephen F. Austin Press, 2014): "she who does not feel her name beneath her feet will wander, will wander" and "where it begins"

Poets Reading the News: "fishbone" and "like fish, like song"

Quick Lightning: "onomasticon (or, I sing the names of our dead)"

Scars: An Anthology, ed. Erin Wood (Et Alia Press, 2015): "scar" (originally published as "of scar, palimpsest")

Split This Rock: "till the taste of free in our mouths (brown baby lullaby)"

Veils, Halos, and Shackles: International Poetry on the Abuse and Oppression of Women, ed. Charles Adés Fishman and Smita Sahay (Kasva Press, 2016): "missionary"

Word Riot: "for the boy who went to war & came back fire, came back song"

Writing the Walls Down: A Convergence of LGBTQ Voices, ed. Helen Klonaris and Amir Rabiyah (Trans-Genre Press, 2015): "the other side (I)" and "the other side (II)"

Yellow Medicine Review: "blood of la Mojana"

Most of the pieces in this collection were first written from 2012 to 2015 within & through life configured by the enervations of autoimmune illness that has left me often bedbound. For how writing has been possible through this & its aftermaths, I am indebted for the creative, intellectual & healing sustenance given by too many to name: my kin & kindred, living & spirit; tutors, darlings & co-pilots in the art of every tiny insurgency, every critical defiance, every labor of mourning, every tender & ferocious sorcery. You know who you are & who you've been: you mean worlds to me. In an effort to name some of what has carried me here, & what continues to carry me, my deep & heart-bursting gratitude:

to the wider reach of family & all the nourishment you've offered across years, for what it is to grow a person: la familia Restrepo Rendón y todos que estamos en nuestras redes, the Rhodes & McManus family, the Baker/Guerri/Laverty family, the Casartellis & Bebouts, the Shaws, the Principes, the Shumakers, the Tuch/Wordes family, Kris & Steve Cope, the Brown family, la familia Urruzmendi/Mele, the McElroys & Brownsteins, the Harris family, the Moore/Newberry family.

to the late but always with me Micael Merrifield, whose wily grin, whose rogue & boundless spirit gathered us round many fires, poetry for breakfast, yourself a house of small & everyday milagros.

for the sustenance-labors of body, heart & everyday life that you gave with love while much of this collection was written: Drake Logan.

for lessons in ferocious intellect & for my first encounters with theoretical languages of haunting as political labor, of mourning as a labor of being *with:* Angana P. Chatterji & Richard Shapiro.

you, brilliant loves & lovelies; familia & rock; witches & kindred; my collaborators & fellow riff-raff; poets & artists, teachers & muses; darlings who have been a source of onward & yes, another eye to my pages, another nod, or nudge, or embrace from near & far & before & after the work never done; my queers & queerly alive; artists, scholars, activists, friends; you who've kept & keep me afloat; who've fed me meals & fed my spirit; who shine much light & offer me place; who share in the heartbreak & want for the world; who listen & show up for the lovework of mutual fortification & expansive liberation; who remind me the blurred boundaries between creative life & justice & healing & love, including: Dana Aleshire, Kay Ulanday Barrett, Herman Bennett, Patty Blum, Sarah Browning, Hector Marino Carabalí, Adele Carpenter, Dale Carter, KJ Cerankowski, Harry Chotiner, jAms Aguila Clabecq, Richard Clark, Fredrick Douglass Kakinami Cloyd, Paisley Currah, Leah Danze, LeiLani Dowell, Kyle Casey Chu/Panda Dulce, Pete Espinosa, Amy Fisher, Miri Gabriel/Maryam Imam, Sarah Rafael García, Eva Goodwin, John Gunderson, Raquel Gutiérrez, Danielle Hartounian, Christian Hawkey, Jessica Hsu, Tala Khanmalek, Ashley Kish, Esperanza Leso, Kenji C. Liu, Davíd Gerardo López Martínez, LeShaun Lovell, Christina Mansfield, Jake Matkov, Chris Mayorga, Mutombo M'Panya, Elizabeth Palmer, Alison Parks, Tanisha Payton, César Ramos, Brahim Rouabah, Annie Segrest, Mauro Sifuentes, Alejandro Urruzmendi, Max Urruzmendi, Shaira Vadasaria, Dan Vera, Vickie Vértiz, Annie Virginia, Shamsher Virk, Milo Ward, Aly Wild, Arhm Choi Wild, Pei Wu; Asma Abbas & the Hic Rosa Collective; Carolyn Lazard, Taraneh Fazeli & the Canaries Collective; Leah Lakshmi Piepzna-Samarasinha & everyone of the 2013 Sacred Texts/Collective Dreams Online Workshop; poets of the Split This Rock 2014 Poetry

Festival; aracelis girmay & poets of the 2018 Great Good News of Your Voice Poetry Workshop; Samiya Bashir, poets of the 2018 VONA Poetry Workshop & the whole VONA fam; the Performing Arts Forum; my Sick & Disabled Queer (SDQ) communities; & my Brooklyn College students who dare to experiment with me in convergences of poetry & politics.

Ada Limón, for seeing in this work a book that could mean something in the world; Francisco Aragón, Eli Bortz, Matthew Dowd, Katie Lehman, Wendy McMillen, Letras Latinas & everyone at University of Notre Dame Press who helped bring this book into being with such generosity & care— thank you for carving out space for Latina/o/x voices; Andrés Montoya, who we lost too soon but whose poetry lights a bright, bright way.

mónica teresa ortiz, for so much I name above, & for how we carry each other in the name of poetry & dreams & our many ghosts; for being one who is there every time, to say yes, write, write, write.

my siblings since your first breathing, for the so many ways we are together an us—cosquis never far, Chelsea Rhodes & Chris Rhodes; you & yours.

& most of all, love y infinite gracias always, to my mamita, Mariela del Rosario Restrepo (Rendón) Rhodes, who is the nest, the warmth of sun, the root that draws me home.

introduction to the poems

There are times we come to poetry to be soothed, lifted, brought back into the cool ease of the self. But, there are also times when we come to poetry to be unhoused from our supposed safety, to be ruined by our own world, to be made to feel what we often tuck away within us in order to survive. Reader, let me tenderly warn you, the clear-eyed, lyrically charged poems in *The Inheritance of Haunting* do the latter. With a muscular music that engages layered repetitions and a sort of breathless lineation, these stunning poems disturb the still waters of the body. And doesn't it feel like a time to be disturbed? To see the world not decorated, but unmasked?

We come to poetry because we are interested in the power of language, which, as Adrienne Rich said, "is the power of our ultimate relationship to everything in the universe," but also because we are aware of its inherent failures.[1] Like history, the dominant language and stories often want the hero to win, the wrongdoings of the colonizer to be dissolved and explained away by "success" or "valor." Heidi Andrea Restrepo Rhodes is not interested in those retold tired stories—she's interested in the truth. With a uniquely intersectional eye (and ear), Rhodes unravels the violence of Colombia's Thousand Days' War, the history of rape culture and femicide, and the weight of carrying historical trauma. These are not easy subjects, and so these are not easy poems.

Still she manages, rather astoundingly, to make truly beautiful, sonically rich poems out of these hard subjects. We might agree that the very act of writing is an act of defiance, survival, rebellion, and what Rhodes is doing here is just that: defiantly singing her poems while revealing the many ghosts underneath our feet. Those ghosts—of the speaker's own grandfathers and grandmothers, of victims of violence, of historical figures—are resurrected here. She writes, "whenever I sing/there are generations in my throat," and almost as if the haunting transforms into a much needed visitation, the dead seem to be entirely present and alive in the poems that pay such keen homage to them.

In a 2014 interview, the famed Chilean poet Raúl Zurita spoke about violence, torture, and the universality of terror, "I think that poetry and art have to narrate those things, to speak them, and at the same time, to believe that they might be able to exorcise them. . . ."[2] Here, I believe, is a great exorcism. These are poems that will get under your skin, stay with you for their lyrical power and their honesty and, dare I say it, they will haunt you. But in that haunting there is also the sweet relief that comes when you have recognized the truth, wrestled with history's pain, and like Rhodes herself, survived and been made stronger. Above all, what you will remember most is the singing. The singing is eternal.

—Ada Limón,
Judge

The Inheritance of Haunting

Haunting is the cost of subjugation. It is the price paid for violence, for genocide. Horror films in the United States have done viewers a disservice in teaching them that heroes are innocent, and that the ghouls are the trespassers. In the context of the settler colonial nation-state, the settler hero has inherited the debts of his fore-fathers. This is difficult, even annoying to those who just wish to go about their day. Radio ads and quips from public speakers reveal the resentment some settlers hold for tribal communities that assert claims to land and tribal sovereignty. This resentment seems to say, "Aren't you dead already? Didn't you die out long ago?"

Erasure and defacement concoct ghosts; I don't want to haunt you, but I will.

— Eve Tuck and C. Ree,
"A Glossary of Haunting,"
Handbook of Autoethnography

Glendower: I can call spirits from the vasty deep.
Hotspur: Why, so can I; or so can any man;
But will they come when you do call for them?
—William Shakespeare, *Henry IV*

Tell me who you haunt and I'll tell you who you are.
—Andre Bréton, *Nadja*

PART I

El Otro Lado/The Other Side

the past is a candle in the temple of my mouth

power of a ghost
in my mouth
in the temple of my mouth
seat of my throat
undertongue, a basket
in which
I carry you.

ghost, my ghost, my precedent,
my beloved revolutions
my beloved lost
show me tomorrow's questions
let me cut my teeth
on their jagged, hopeful edge

the other side (I)

to see behind walls, delved vessels, diluting pretense,
majestic interludes dissolving grim partitions, feet on ruins
bulwarked in the name of sanctuary, or preemptions,

we map ourselves by the light of hesitancies & moon,
piece by piece, layer by layer
against the immurements of this age, the suffocations
of mandates, the endorsements of our corseting, we never
feel the fullness of we, of our fine-tuned strange,
these edicts clothing us, asphyxiating the tender shine
of our scarlet radiance, secrets, the pouring forth of marvel, &

I run my fingers over cold broken pieces, brick, rubble,
like tablets speaking four thousand commandments
of loving in a time of tombstones declaring
the beauty of,   like the grinding of rocks between our molars,
we suck the bones of our caging, tongues seeking marrow, hungry for,
hungry for, hungry for,   &

I run my fingers over my cheeks, walls holding in teeth,
                                          holding in words,
every letter of every name, the old names of our want, the quiet names &
raucous names of every staggering loneliness,
the pittance of company behind
an abundance of divisions, doors,

with the flame of your teeth you scale me, climbing over me searching
for what was on my other side: the side of dreams, the side of
unleashed compositions, balladry, song,
the side signed "x," illiterate or uncharted, peculiar,

I lean my ear up to it all, & trace
the soft worn years holding it all in beneath the audibility of screams

& that place where the stones have worn
from your years of knocking

scar

sleeping at the base hairline back of my neck, it is quiet,
I forget it is there until a lover runs those lips up my scapula
over the C1 vertebrae, toward my ears, & there, an inquiry lands
atop my lobes, fetching after the story of this blemish,
          distressed skin at my nape,
       left.

scar lingers like a ghost traversing generations: the stitched mouth
birthmark in place as my mother's, & her mother's, &
I don't know how many mothers before her,
there, below my globe skull,
rendering its own geographies beneath furtive histories, waver
in my dreams like apparitions,
carved out of me by scalpel to avoid the blight of
malignancies on its horizon.

scar whispers ancient tales, far away places, & old world sorceries
that hex the branches of families or cover them
in incantatory armors. Somewhere,
my dna, ours, has stored the story. (perhaps) a war & a firing squad, or
the hunt of witches, & a bullet from behind
that pierced the cerebellum, cursing
our line with the interruption of equilibrium,
bestowing on us the disease of
v − e − r −
        t − i − g −
                o,
embedding the dizzy of genocides.

(perhaps) an amulet burned into the skin, worn ambiguity over years
centuries of disuse, which at some time shielded our ancestors
from the savage condemnations of a colonial army. (perhaps) the coded
branding
of a hieroglyphic secretly awakened
our senses in every lifetime,

to another possible world & the defiance of
gilded patriarchies.

a trace of things we cannot remember,   semblance
of unwritten. evidence without record. remnant of ferocities,
trauma. palimpsest plotted out in the hull: of horrors we survived, or
the invocation of letters that harbor us in sanctuary through the ages.

my finger sketches its boundaries, small country of wound, murmuring
of rumors from the riddle nevus, its inklings, its estimations,

archive of our old mothers

& their treacherous strides.

all your braids like a compass will bring us home

During the colonial period in Colombia, the hairstyles of black slaves were used
as a secret code to communicate the routes to freedom, allowing many
to reach the palenques, or free settlements, built and populated by escaped slaves.

1. this is the work of mothers: harvest tobacco, cotton, cane. memorize the mountainside
   what embraces it between the farms & haciendas. smile at el Jefe. mine for gold.

                                    gather, gather.

                        gather in the courtyard women & girls in the late afternoon,
                        for the hour of combing. Secret languages passed around like bread.

2. the fingers are a comb. the comb is a machete. the comb is a shield. the comb is a sorcerer's
   feather concealing in its teeth the devices of our escape.

3. secret maps woven like baskets,   (harboring seeds & gold crumbs)
   code slipping under the eye of the beast,   oil this scalp, this breathing papyrus,
                        patience child, we need your holy head.

4. fathers, brothers, listen closely. watch so you will know the way.
                        we are the cartographers of our liberation.

5. forehead to nape. this is how you read. this is how we arm you in the language of threads.

6. knot, braid, knot, bow, braid, knot / tallest tree, road, a sowed field of screaming seeds,
   turn left at the orchard, more road, hide inside this trunk,

                        the old ceiba tree will curl its roots around you, a watchful grandfather.

7. these rows like trenches: watch for the sludge of swamps. beware caimans, feral dogs,
   gunshots, snakebites. beware la Tunda!

8. (resistencia, hope with feet. a smile can be a treacherous thing. have you seen the fire in
   our blood? Have you seen these eight legs?

   two hands to the plow, & six to chart the underground.)

9. row, knot, braid, knot, knot, bow, braid, knot / river, mango, road, plátano, a rock
   shaped like Ananse, a steep & winding path, a meadow leading to refuge where your
   uncle waits for you tonight.

10. your hair, daughter,
    is the meadow I crouch in,

    tu pelo, mija, my North Star,
    the twined rope road pulling me home.

    your hair, daughter, black & ferocious,
    your hair, cunning & defiant,
    your hair, beautiful, whispers in tressy tongues.

    your brazen braids
    give me the taste of free in my mouth.

11. the net, the seashell,
    the petals of flowers or moon,
    borderlands, wild pigs
    & trails of hyacinth
    dappling the dirt
    like hushed mouths divulging red,
    drumming out the twists & turns
    of overgrown footpaths:

    hold still, darkest sleep, we are not coming to you yet.

12. hold still, child, let me weave a song through, & bring the shelter of gods to your feet.
    let me part the soil from the hank
    the water from the road.

13. we are spiders under the cover of lock,
    fugitive atlas, coil & crown.

all that is left

I excavate the epigenetic residue, strata of history & its traumas.
hue of my uncle's arms wrapped around me,
tracing my fingers around cigarette & clove
follicles embedded in his, epidermal storying
speaks quiet declarations, of the Black Atlantic & severed gods,
ruptured prayer, jungle ghosts, genealogies left behind in the struggle
to survive in a land where white was beauty, & power,
& all that was solid, enough in the eye's eye.

my grandfather is the lightest of his, his white papery
skin translucent in the sun, no cinnamon umber.
he regales me with tales
of youth, love,
always love, & the beauty of my grandmother,
(reminding me, again) forbidden to see him, who
liked to drink his a little too much: that is the story he tells.

my grandmother, however much
she flung her obedience into the mountainside
to hold hands through a cracked window
till the violet hours of dusk, insisted
the disfavor lay in skin-time, wiry hair,
the Black of Black, the Brown of Brown,
(sus)staining roots & he either denies this,

or does not remember. or never knew.

does not remember,
does not remember

the songs they wrapped him in,
their medicine eucalyptus leaf chicken feet
history of histories that held the nest for life itself
stored in their gums, wounds of mourning & ever the fight.

remembers white
was the cream of his love's cheek.
published in the imaginary of his deliverance, white
was the reach to providence & provision; white was
the solidity of stucco walls keeping out the wind;
color virtue, Jesus
hanging from the cross. white
was access & accomplishment;
escape from dust & sweat of farming & illiteracy. white was
honor & chivalry; sex; the robust muscle of
industry in the castle of the metropolis.

heaves the lacuna, dragging it through the city,
kissing it into the ears of his children, & somewhere,
beneath the shade of orange bricks & Devil's Breath,

it is lost:

the archive & chronicling, of sound & sense,
skin & song, a generation's becoming in the aria of seizure,
rent from the root,
born in the rot & tumble of conquest's inheritance,
the multitude of death & exhalations, the rationing of extance:

white was & does not remember,

all left of memory

is skin.

where it begins

it is easy
to walk into a room
full of
white people
& feel

ugly.

it begins with feeling / Strange /
& all the tutorials / of letters & billboards, hateful / epicureans,
curators of glamour / shunning the stain /

every history scribed / into our skin, of cane / carving trees /
on our grandmothers' grandmothers' backs / like branches
at the edge of their spines /

yes, it begins
with feeling strange / like wild birds who choked / for centuries, on tales
of horror, monsters / architected from our eyeballs & sinew /
our fingernails worn by scratching the walls / of our immurements, gas chambers,
forced musicalities / digging from the earth / the graves for our own dismembered
generations / dripping winged, clawed, hair slithering straight with venom / black
& night-worn, yes,

this is where it begins.

it begins with the alphabet / of mannerisms cloaked in propriety /
the orthopedics of recollection / eugenics & moral decay, enunciating
our wrong-boned & dreadful / & all the heinous reminders of brutal /
these houses were built on / the bondage stinking breath / violet bricks
    built of blood /

it begins with a map gone wrong / flung into cartographies of suspicion /
    wrought
into conventions / adulations of impeccability /

so we, this mess, cross the doorjamb / we are greeted with a smile /
& all the endlessness of years piled up / to remind us / this gnarl tooth
blossomed / from a root that runs too deep to measure

tristeza profunda

when they lobotomized my tía abuela,
it was for the immensity of her sadness
la tristeza profunda,
nació before she even breathed in this world,
born before the Thousand Days' War,
when her tío's tío's head was sent home in a box,
born before those lands had been aojado,
by the long eyes of gun barrels
transpiercing warriors flying like birds
born before chains & contracts & Atlantic Trade.

her tears tangled
the governing, doctors, priesthood, police,

smaller & smaller
spaces between
distraught,
disorderly,
delirium
   danger.

hidden in the blossoming Andes
inside those walls buttressed by sweat
a stationed eye
ignoring centuries of violence
endless desecrations with their infinite implications,
birthing madnesses disseminated across
generations
oceans
& brave singing years.

they said
deranged animal, demons no prayer could extinguish
under science of reason & reason of science: two faces of one God.

disarranged her memory
so that fifty years later
the rest of us could not find our way
home without maps
drawn in a foreign king's tongue.

felled her melancholy to harvest docility
planting kernels, insolence pounding the earth in uproar,
axis of all the sadnesses that despaired before,
before the Thousand Days' War,
before she was fixed, vacuous torpor,
before memory was scraped from our insides
leaving nothing but stench of rotting guava.

not the sun alone blanches our skin, breaks our hearts beneath the heat
but our vehemence speaks more than one language,
our vociferations are the bleeding echoes of voices silenced before:

shadows underneath shambles of her once radiant sense & wit
carry us as on a raft towards the mouth of remembrance
down the tendrils of the Río Cauca.

heard in the yes of gods

black charcoal around her eyes
intended to ward off the blue-eyed horror:
of conquest, & Old World logic,
imperial demons, & wretch,
who reached for fortune of skin & stone;
dissecting their coming into cursed oblivion
shielding her from the hands of denigration & trespass.

It was not heard in the yes of gods,

unbelieving in imprecations or the sacred—
reason waved away all hesitation:
taking sanctified by throned fists
& all death, ancillary to the devices of prosperity, property

though doubt traced furrowed brows:
they could not shake such nausea of frailty,

the sense, that from behind a rock somewhere,
eyes were watching, whispering prayers
heard in the yes of gods, prayers
that could pierce the brawn of a thousand blades
with the backbone of jaguar nights & centuries of a "New World" ichor.

she who does not feel her name beneath her feet will wander, will wander

home is not
           voice
rendering me miniscule
beneath the infinitely resounding
boom of his needs

not the uncanny
of my body
shriveling into corners
when the rooster crows

not the sad & ugly
run of replicated stone
between grassy expanse

home is not
white, white,
everywhere

forgotten idioms,
the periled trajectories
of divided romances,
the heroics of bloodshed
the terror of ash
muddled in my mix

it is not
the go back where you came from
when there is nowhere but here,
the close-range sting of
hockey puck in my sister's spine
& five hundred years of

but we belong here too

if I wear my hair this way

mija, if I wear my hair / wrapped in a bun this way / like a cyclops full moon / or the tidy nest of a colibrí / it means the day was long in grave caverns / it means I spent the hours eating mud / scouring the under-earth for light & glimmer / it means my blistered feet will ache by the fire & I will have no words for you tonight /

pero mija, if you see my hair let loose / suelto, unleashed / like a crown of wild spiral crows / or a fishing net full of flying sable salmon / it means the hours passed while I panned in the shallow edges of a cool spring / gazing into the batea / it means your smile came to me / a glistening sun in the silver sifting plate / it means tonight I will knit my arms around you / I will open my ears to your monsoon of questions / I will sing you the holy songs of trees /

imbunche

—(after Catalina Parra)

you've heard the tales
of the child, the child, the child
taken in the night

lips sewn shut with sinew of cattle
under fluorescent glow, authoritarian sorceries,
fire of interrogation lamps, impunity,
incantations demanding silence
beneath arms broken & bound, bones
relinquishing testimony under the spell
of the hammer

you've heard, they damned
orifices of the crying,
suturing senses into silence;
slicing the tongue
confining its stories to cavities
between the teeth
to blinding darkness
forced erasures
sculpting the obscene bird of night
like paper snowflakes
dyed in mute blood
the secrecy of hemoglobin
dried on the floors of torture centers
fashioned from schools, these

cursed caves inhabited by
              crowns
woven filaments
turned silver in a day
by the alchemies
of unbridled governance.

you've heard the tale
of the child
who was taken in the night, the night, the night

fed flesh of babies
milk
transfigured from human ground
into underworld of the beast,
beaten by the sacralization
of brutality, regimes of forgetting
under years
transformation under abuse
& the exile of memory
under the sinister magic of despotism.

you've heard the stanzas of
brujo dictatoris
feeding off the abominable

you've heard
the conjurings,
citizens who wept
for the nameless, the mother
who named the missing,
the missing whose protests
struck the public ear
then disappeared like lightning,
the nameless who gagged on their future
beneath the soil of unmarked graves,
the supplications for regard from
a world bustling with magpies

&
the architects who knew
the refutations, denunciations of their crimes
would only be quieted & quit
by removing the heart,
cutting off the head
of the child-beast
imbunche
& calling it demon

1901

hustled the mines,
cavernous, carnivorous
depths glimmering precious
in the façade of their dreams.

abundance never theirs to keep,
(neither their dreams),
save for the dust-shimmer
that travelled home with them,
in their hair, & the fibers
of their sweat-stained cotton shirts.

my grandfather's grandfather's grandfather
slogging for gold & quartz
while the Thousand Days' War
trudged on;
men swallowed by the depths
of trembling Andes earth-loam
if not first slain, while
heads rolled down hillsides
so the aristocracy can
keep polishing their claws
on all things shiny.

blood of la Mojana

heard tell
something
paradisiacal,
gates inviting passage
a twinkling,
having traversed the mighty sea
searching
cities of gold, tired men missing their mothers.

Official History
wrote us
as if bellicose savagery
to which they, victim
flailing beneath our carnivorous teeth,
one by one,
fallen to the death-hand
of our pantheistic New World Hades.

wrote their generals & kings
of brutal drownings their crew
mesmerized by brown-skinned girl
creatures feathers in hair
fishbones through nostrils;
soldiers down,
pulled deep into the Orinoco
by winged maiden pirañas
riding on the backs of caimans.

plotted cartographies of desecration
& did not call it genocide;
named our trees other names,
strangling us riverweed pulled
from shallow banks,
crucified our fathers
in thorned crowns woven of cat's claw,
piercing swords our children,
whose small bodies reflected in the glassy river-table
grew anaconda tails where legs had once,

wrapping tight around
the scourge of invasion
muscles clenched with shock of upheaval
asphyxiating
these puppet aggressors
to the point of collapse:
this was survival.

had come from afar
to desiccate, defecate
our lands,
dilute memory,
decimate thousands
of moon horizons we'd bathed.

their want & dread of an angry god,
transfiguring our tributaries
into an unmarked carmine liquid tomb,
drawing the curtain over an era:

we could no longer swim
without swallowing
the feverish wails of lost children.

seven generations/one

you wound up, always, face flat
to the ground, empty bottle
falling out of your apron pocket
looking to fill itself with stones
or the shred of secret dreams, desires,
the old countryside legends
carried in the beaks of crows, left
unintelligible in the strain of their caw.

your skin weathered by spells
of a melancholy noonday sun weighing down
your eyelids through the nightmares
you winced at from behind the gloss of your
clouded sky irises, lost hours,
your children calling your name, telling time
by stalk shadows & the echoing
of your blur against the husks, wondering
if your flesh would be pecked come morning.

what agonies swirled your watering gums,
what gnawed your lips,
what flask sorrow devoured you before
the crickets had even begun their shank chorus?

I see you there
a quilt of soil patterning your hem,
dry rotgut crusted on your lips
desiccating their injured underground.

I look for you in the cornfields,
wondering if the worms have yet found your ears.

the flower husband

abuela's ghost
breathes, azalea plant, veins reaching
pocket of sunlight that catches the wall
in early afternoons while babies sleep
to songs of venderos out in the street
selling wishes &   aguacate, aguacate

abuelo still tends to it
thirteen years after she, gone
quenches its mornings
scent of coffee, arepas, wafting near windows
brings delight, memories of children running barefoot
through the halls, the banter & wisecracks of siblings,
the softly swaying to boleros, close enough to hear
a belly's quiet rumble

shows me faded photographs
from his closet, a cache of angels he keeps
under lock & key, dutiful steward of reminiscences,
his brother who disappeared during la Violencia,
my cousin who drowned despite
the boding & augur that grazed our sleep,
& there, his true love, unaltered grace
held between his fingers, enamored still:
first moment beauty ravished his equilibrium
his ballast in the boundless night.

grown blind from the weathering of years,
his eyes sparkle for her, moon on broken glass
& azalea, still blooms,   a single
once a year come spring, clockwork & when,
he bends to inhale fragrant poems
summon his yearning,
tips the quiet into his ears catch a milky whisper
brushing lip to petal, renewing his vows,

devoted flower husband

how she flourishes beneath his cheek,
redolent joy of yesterdays
& I wonder, when his time comes, wither,
will the last blossom fall, or will there two
where once one, radiant,
unfurled its secrets for her lover's flesh?

purgatory

—*(for Luisa)*

nobody talks about how
after you died,
your hallway portrait hanging
cried salty,
dripping down the frame,
wetting the discount wallpaper

nobody talks about the fifth hand
that grieved no longer feeding
the child's spoon-covet mouth,
about how a portrait does not eat,
about how another witness was wanted
to testify the impossibility
of pigment & linseed in whimper

how this could not
have happened, have happened, for
if you were wall & weeping
what of heaven?
little babies called home
do not go to Purgatory
from suckle's swell & milk:
or that is what the priest said.

when a child awakens
again & again
to announce her coming death
to sound the nightmare alarm & trial
what is to be done?

how every rock-a-bye
becomes a prayer
divining interlude
a parent's unrelenting sorcery
family revelation

let me cull the storehouse of sorrow,
how the purgatory was not you, prima,
not your wide-eye briny weeping walls,
your keen infant blue

but the footsteps, the stair,
your father wandering
globe of his ache, haunted
call & burden, nights of teeth ground
counting the slipped minute

it was licking the wall to find you,

the years of anticipating
your wailing in the next room,

knowing it would never come.

la Llorona

—(after San Juan Capistrano and its ghosts who also grew me up)

run when you hear
shrill stone pellet voice pounding the night,
where the wood of your front door been scraped,
where scratched through the moonless,
beware her wrath, her loneliness, keep your children close,
away from the edges waters: even the crayfish run
(warnings etched in dust under scabbed bark
old pepper tree down, or under
hyperbole of generations or Hollywood)

ghost of la Llorona roams, but
filling the creek centuried tears
mother's ache swirling madness of the nightwall she roams

braids brazenly sway
beat of ancient drum, bleeding corazón
a midday swallow dying in her hand
& she cries & she cries & she cries & she cries

beneath the horror of slow massacres
                            along the sweep of these majestic geographies
beneath the sweat & blisters, chain,
tethered cattle & their leathered scars
broken bones under bricks building houses for a strange & brutal god
beneath the knife throb tormenting her inviolable violable

beneath the grasp of the children she drowned, beloved
dwellers of womb
sleeping in the sanctuary of waters,
tucked silted gravel-bed by her unraveled hands
beneath the long survival of her misery, days
hiding beneath head-tall mustard flowers beneath fury
& mayhem of her longing just to smell their hair once more

her crying is sorrow her crying is prayer her crying is
empty cradle arms & rage of boundless years bellied up
beyond these two thousand graves, names seeded gravelly
(*trabuco* is a thunder-gun, a prick, a word for *through the belly*)

her crying is a mother an age standing at the edge of
mother water time

whose children buried by their own teeth
save them from the sour jagged perforations of unjust bondage, or

whose children died in the violence of, in the violence of, in the violence,
whose children died in violence, whose children died, whose children
died
whose children

the dream in which we die together

is always changing, but dark,
night has fallen on the era,
we weep between our toes
running from a gun
whose barrel-tongue
bears our names

we rush in the shadows
of bridges, leaving fragments,
ink like bread crumbs, wondering
if the sea will steal our footprints
from the sand, leaving us traceless

but then I awaken
to your gently sleeping eyelids,
their stop-motion blossoming
into the day
& it is now, I know

these three hundred lives we lived
reaching out like finger bones
to remind us
how hard we fought
for here, this simple morning.

missionary

colonization sticky,
residue, viscid, layering my aorta,
pulsing through my blood,
from hypothalamus to labial nerve,
deep beyond years beyond the days I've breathed beyond centuries
beyond the rapes of my grandmothers' grandmothers' grandmothers

colonization sticky,
how wholly hands took to beat, crushed children
cathedrals could be built, souls could be saved

in a world already
language of god in the soil & sound of jungle birds
harvesting of corn & plantain
priests staked their claim
planted crosses like dead trees
that feigned to give eternal life
impaling the blood of the earth
impaling my body
centuries into a future they could not foretell.

& they told my grandfathers
how to fuck their women
for the glory of god
& what once were
potent dancing flowers
fierce with skilled weapons in their skirts

became in their eyes
machines to make more slaves,
slave-factories
before factories were factories

& oh how my grandmothers bled
& fought
& died
& refused to die
(for I am here)

drip,   wet,
this residue between my legs,
five hundred years of history
I carry between my legs,
in my bones,
stories carved against my will
with the pointed tip of a tagua rosary

the heresy in our bones

—(after Fanon)

this, we were made to believe,
this, hammered into our marrow,
this unspeaks us from the primary kernel bleeding off the lip:
we germ rot.
cosmic effluvia, stench of biblical proportion.
we crumb-land,
land for bread, not landed, bread in hand.
we animal, we stain,
we mudded blister recessing to the nub.
we grown our own, seeded long time far,
we taken root & sprung from the very water of our bowels
these trees from which we spin infernal circle, pendulum under branch:
we our skin, shadowed catastrophe,
swarthy dread & grave, we swallowed the decrepit note
crumbling way down to the gag, we
burn our fingers trying, call each scar a perfect stone.

this, now, this:
no home like we, no time like now,
no refuge for precisions so diligently laid out by masons of then,
we fill the underground, we pound the lung like drum,
we catch the force of cry to sing the night, stitch the sting from our backs
we holler our names in the moonless,
we the sun, we lightning flash-bang burning fire,
we beast the lingering order, we underscore our glorious mayhem,

we the splendor, we life & death & dark & day,
we fracture these acres under thrall, like
Big Bang, brutal emergence, like we
birthing ourselves lashing the violent cage,
sourcing a rise from barren hope, piecemeal, we come:
ferocious, cutthroat dawn.

prayer for the children who will be born with today's daggers in their tomorrow eyes

these five hundred years in our bones
striated conquistas dragging
the letters of the harrowed tongue
into the geography
of our marrow, down,
                          down
these armas in the arms of little, dragging
blood across the pupil dilating moonshadow
breathing in   history with light,
portraits of departed hearts, singing
streets, the greed under the floorboards,
libraries of the broken,
amassing names we carve,
unpredictable weather patterns leaving
splinters where our mothers' houses
once stood, rotten mountains of perfect food
rustled up in the company of flies, & madness,
empty oceans   homeless starfish,
the severing of limbs, trees, human fists like
thunder, & vacant motherhoods grasping
at apparitions

& we, we puncture the words we are
teaching you   with
every revelation every bit every chain
we have failed to release & burn
we perforate the dawn before it even knows
it has skin,   so

take this palm, this love, this firehunger
see what second sight will sigh
in your winding direction, unpeel your
soot-stained eyelids from the corpse parade
& run it through, run it through

find the tomorrow we could not give you.

the other side (II)

this wall of bones, chapel of memory ossified,
stacked femur columns, the oblivion of gold in the crevices of teeth,

skeletal arches, metacarpal daisies, & mud,
ghosts whispering appellations, forgotten, last spoken in the wind of
long ago midnights, or yesterday
the delicacy of skin, muscle, tendons,
frailty of bodies rent under the edges of occupation,
tired resistance, future rage coded into the chromosomes of our birthing,

tonight I weep for the children who were my cousins, grandmothers,
five hundred years old, stacked into the pillars of churches
to fortify mud & straw sheltering priests & kings from
the torrent of jungle rain & the violent mourning wax palm canopies,

tonight I stand how many thousands of miles away, across borders,
distant geographies, the other side
of our wayward memory, the other side of hells you lived,
the other side of bone-walls, ghosts breathing onomastic tales,
wailing grief, the bitterness of broken ribs,

I kiss your lips, & remember their names, there too,
your teeth room the chronicling of violence,
of your grandmothers, of genocides
cracked sidewalks, skulls, split lips
of today's antagonisms, & all the contempt
of righteous boots, fists

there, in a kiss, we scale the wall of bones, we scale our own teeth, facing
our dismemberments through mnemonic histories, there
in the crevices of concrete, from ash, from the wreckage of centuries,

small yellow flowers, bougainvilleas blanketing stone, arias of freedom,

we scale the ache to bloom home.

¿Qué somos?, me preguntaste una semana o un año después,
¿hormigas, abejas, cifras equivocadas
en la gran sopa podrida del azar?
Somos seres humanos, hijo mío, casi pájaros,
héroes públicos y secretos.

———

What are we? you asked a week or year later,
ants, bees, wrong numbers
in the big rotten soup of chance?
We're human beings, my son, almost birds,
public heroes and secrets.

—Roberto Bolaño, "Godzilla in México,"
trans. Laura Healy

PART II

Casi Pájaros / Almost Birds

dis-astre

these events, ourselves
asunder, exiled from our stars,
our guides, sightless night
shorn by our every
miniscule apocalypse, atoms
like planets breaking, misfortunes
tethering regret, the failure of inoculations,
the collapse of disbelief, shredded altitudes
fretting our sense of upward, out

the plundered remembrance
that home was a star that glittered
in shining sounds of fiddlers rustling,
that day was a star, & mother, & prayer,
& every god who fed us
the bursting forth of seedlings under rain,
& also tomorrow, stars, all,
luminescing constellation, out of reach
from beneath the sprouting grasses,
from under earth, from the never-breath lung

until midnight dogs
dirty their jaws, & like howling
feral midwives, endure the hours
heaving the gravel of torments in the
delivery of bones, the birthing of claims,
the gift of illumination
impossible in the stench of withered sockets
under the light of ancient suns
their yet
unannounced & holy extinguishing.

when the machete will sever the ballad
(memory-mourning for El Mozote)

*There was one in particular the soldiers talked about that evening . . . a girl on
La Cruz whom they had raped many times during the course of the afternoon,
and through it all . . . this girl had sung hymns, strange evangelical songs, and
she had kept right on singing, too, even after they had done what had to be
done, and shot her in the chest. She had lain there on La Cruz with the blood
flowing from her chest, and had kept on singing—a bit weaker than before,
but still singing. And the soldiers, stupefied, had watched and pointed. Then
they had grown tired of the game and shot her again, and she sang still, and
their wonder began to turn to fear—until finally they had unsheathed their
machetes and hacked through her neck, and at last the singing had stopped.*
—Mark Danner, "The Truth of El Mozote,"
New Yorker, December 6, 1993

it is December &
there will be light
somewhere shining
from the god of ravens
& Jesus, maguey, youth,
there will be
light shining
out of the mouths
of moon silversides
defying their slippery gravity
to leap their testimony at the moon,

the others wrestle shrill with
their own endings,

barely she moves
but sings her prayer,
barely she moves
her back to the damp
soil of the hill
turn by turn
these soldiers
            invade

scorched earth tarring their hearts,

inviting the vultures to breakfast:
Atlacatl is disgraced.

barely she moves,
but sings amidst the detritus
of broken glass bottles
a battalion rendered weary

guaro stinging her cuts
force of despoilment
rhythming her small body
a hard thunder in her ears,

she sings, she sings

melodies to the clouds above her,
beckoning the wrath of angels
genealogies of pain, traces
of wraiths & torment upon the slumber
of questioning guns,
she sings,

she sings.

barely she moves,
but she sings.

she sings in tongues
the names of grandmothers,
haunts the suspicion of soldiers,
beneath the bullet, the chorus trembling

they call her demon,
again, again,
beneath lead
they aim to assuage fear rising
in their veins, of demons & loss,
nugatory pull in the gut,
memories of their own sisters,
an aching for home, hung
out of reach,
like the children
in the field below,
swaying beneath the blood
of branches sapping
the taste of disbelief.

barely she moves,
but still she sings,

the incantation
that will confess the day
to the wind,
sympathy
of the stars,

still she sings,

until the last moment
when the machete
will sever the ballad,

until the last moment,

she sings,

she sings

until the last moment.

charred skulls of children sleep piled in the earth
in the corner of the sacristy,
housing beetles & the roots of dandelions:

a quiet wrenches itself from hiding.

fog

accumulation
of goats, pigeons, heaped
succumbed to rigor mortis
the gloom of final days,

day is quiet, eerily, fending off
irrevocability

the boughing of trees unescorted by
chirping, streets vending only the
strange light of midday sifted
through dust & the residue of wailing

this child, curled in her father's arms
who now looks smaller than she has ever been,
who gasped for sky to tell him
"today, it is my sister's turn to eat,"
before choking on the vacuum of answers

she sleeps the boundless sleep
like the others
cold, immobile on the ground, children
like little birds all in a row, dreaming
the dawn of their infinite soundlessness
capitulated to the fog in their lungs

no nests of chandeliers,
crystal green shimmering,
these unwanted deaths
of the blameless, the finale
of a fleeting prayer
that winged & walked
on small legs,

only yesterday laughing at the absurdity
of cloud-shapes, only yesterday
singing aspirations of
metamorphosis,
only yesterday, unsettled & buoyant
amid the inheritance
of erosions & loss.

last balloon

—(after My Feelings about the War,
    watercolor by Vietnamese refugee, age 12)

when every balloon has popped, burst,
pricked by the fervent fire pounding
piercing night

explosions like needles
death's ruby river flooding alleys
day melting pink

when the rain of swift & hasty silver gods shining,
gust of lead dirigibles crashing,
fill sky with ash,
our mothers wrench their mouths
into sirens over our dying & their splintered limbs

purple stained aprons, wet infinite crumbling
our family flesh, every mute breath a valediction

I run to tag you, I sprint,
I am the wind crippling under rainbow skin,
catching nine years of screaming
Laos in my mouth on the way,
& our own three million dragged
siblings asunder, bitter flies
on a windshield tongue, I run to tag you,
the fading ray of sunshine an alarm
on my flush cheek, brother
I run to catch you, to sweep you under shelter
with the sea of my arms,
every joy, ruptured latex in the gutter

my father floats, bobbing in the sky,
the last balloon of my youth.

eternal return

this is a madness: liminality, tightrope
neck must also walk, endlessness, waiting,
purgatories handed out like fruit baskets
to mothers sewing hope to the hems
of their dresses so they will not leave it behind
in the dust of their heels
redundant days under the force of sun
sweat beads glistening with visions & ache

my son,
       she prays to no one in particular, or to a god,
       or to lost neighbors (will it matter to whom? did it ever?)

where is he?   questioning the uniformed
desiccated futility of droughts,
       biding time with disbelief,
               rage that also impales her
our sons,
       they implore shut doors of concrete buildings, or a god,
         or each other for the thousandth time,

where where where   this is a fate one cannot love

& the boys in nearby Soacha? they were never uniformed,
what use does a farmer's son have for a uniform?

these are not their weapons, nor these wounds
the night in their eyelids too early fallen, & for how long
did their mothers call out to the sunless sky
their small & mortal names?

weight of absence looms, fatality of forfeiture
claws at the night-door of wondering in the hours between
dark & darker, shadows & negative space lingering in hallways,
        ghosts who flitter in the warm-blooded memories
        held to a mother's breast in fists clenching rusted frames
        broken glass, the chiming of bells calling up the names
        of the ones who never came home for dinner

in the morning, the silence would echo contemptuously
but for the parrot in the rafters
rejoining chorus of lamentations,

    ¿dónde están?
    ¿dónde están?

so far

bare feet scalded by asphalt
holes, soles of her shoes
hottest of days,
does not recognize herself
this dress woven of exhaustion
from threads survival,
exiled into the streets
three children by her side
one on the way

balming scabs deracination
bits of aloe from the public park
hand outstretched to plea
in the name of Mary
so her children may not
wrestle the beast
gnaws at the insides
on the in-between days,
days of mud & puddles, listlessness,
sweat, & empty pockets, holes
burnt with eyes
turned haste of fear,
self-servitude, & the criminal wince
of poverty molded by the close-fisted
artistries
of the gilded.

dreams of home,
when stillness fell from the mountainside
to sing the day down to sleep,
& mornings ripe plantain & papaya,
coffee & cacao,
rang bright with rays of sun
through palms,

when farming was work
when farming was prayer
when farming was breath,
the buoyancy of memory, satiation,
& the growing bones of hers
sprouting to the sky
seeds planted in the soil of generations,
grandfathers tilling tomorrows
with the flavor of fullness.

but these are the days of uproot,
days of threat & disposability,
gunfire & operations,
days of losing & lost,
of river graves & bloody absence,
of brothers unaccounted for.

yes, these are the days of uproot,
days of wanting,
of swallowing the excuses of
helping hands, so-called
these are the days of choosing
who will eat & when,
donations of agencies,
rations of flour
mixes with water,

& spoons to her fledglings
hoping the proteins
of ancestral reminiscence
will catch on the late
afternoon breeze
& stick to their ribs
to carry them
another day
so far, so far,
from the nest.

the terror of clean

that space between
a limpieza & sweeping your kitchen
with a dirty broom, clogged with hair & dust mites
is very, very small, or so they would have you believe.

list of items in a cleaning kit:

    1. broom
    2. soap
    3. brillo
    4. machete
    5. Kalashnikov Modernized Automatic Rifle (AKM) or IMI Galil
    6. shovel

it is Colombia, the 1990s, it is now.

the scrape of nation-building
rendering pillage heroic by
a placid discourse of bourgeois mediocrity:
the exceptional or eccentric is dangerous,
did you not hear? did you not learn it from the inception
of your breathing?

    aporophobia: fear of & contempt toward people who live in poverty.

& these are the disposables, the unwanted, the extraneous bodies, unprofitable,
irrelevant to the march of silver & gold, the laborious privileges of citizenship,
these are the ones who will catch the intention of lavish purges
& be forced to swallow ammo too big for the throat.

kill list for Mano, elusive pervasive hand of death,
another piece of the putrid machinery that governs, that declares from the pit
of unchurched wholly taking, all the sins in their deadliness:

1. foundlings, those with no nest, the homeless. poverty is a sin. sloth
   is a sin.
2. nightwalkers selling their tongues like wares. sex outside marriage
   is a sin.
3. false eyelashes & skirts on a cock-strut, transgender, transvestite,
   transgressing bodies in a militarized culture. deviation from
   masculinity is a sin.
4. faggots & lesbianas. homosexuality is a sin.
5. human rights activists. speaking out is a sin. anti-imperialism is a sin.
6. skin the color of earth & sunless hours. refusing assimilation is a sin.
7. mothers & daughters. mourning is a sin. remembering is a sin.

police with their muddy heels in stirrups on badged horses
talk their talk of cleaner streets, boasting of revelatory
enterprise, bastion cities of order, security sacrosanct,

    so the suits can take trains without trouble
    & the young women of El Poblado, Comuna 14
    can walk their unblemished cheeks & poodles down the sidewalks
    without risking

the tainted guilt of beggarly hands
or the unfamiliar succulence of arousal,

we are the vermin here.

we are the edged blades of fallen yearning,
struck as with lightning & thunder
for all the labyrinthine meanderings of our days
away from the death of a thrust docility,

& we pay for our refusal of purity,
we pay for the distress of their daughters' lips
reaching for ours at sunset in the parks littered
with deviants, our deviations carrying their discomfort,

we pay for not being able to pay, we pay for having been
boys who wore their mothers' heels when she was away
working her third job in one twirl of the sun, we pay for
letting our nucleus grieve, for clipping our roses for hawking
in moonlit markets, for fighting the deepest
fight we can muster in the face of oblivion & contempt,   for

that space between
a limpieza & sweeping your kitchen
with a dirty broom, clogged with hair & dust mites
is very, very small, or so they would have you believe.

watch out,   they will
sweep you into the gutter
& bury you with all the refuse,
tattered clothing, scrap metal, broken radios
of a convoluted wartime sensibility
in the afterglow of an immaculate sterility,

leaving your teeth to shine in the rain.

A11728

—(for Pearl)

she called it *organizing,*
the stealing of bread in Auschwitz,

organized from the kitchen
twelve-hour shifts, in between
hunger straining fortitude, pulling
skin tight against the ribs, her ladle
slipping the more to the needing.

millstone of memory startling sleep,
dreams of the very last day ever, ever, ever,
that mother would be mother & home would be home

summer dress too light for grim of snow
no socks, no coat; a will against the winter
& solidarity in suffering, cohesions threatened
against shattering, face of brutal atrocity
faith

seen death up close:
sweat of the death-train; march toward extinction;
all the pressing degradations serrated by the daggers of opprobrium;
young girl's body, limp
could not be saved by the small piece of bread placed under her tongue.

always ways to fight, she says
means with which to cling
to life, even quiet & small:
an extra piece of bread in the pocket
under the talons
of unending & ravenous starvation

is never, never small.

non-combat related incidents & other lies

—*(for Pfc. LaVena Johnson, July 27, 1985–July 19, 2005)*

there was no ballad
for you in Balad, no
eulogy tending your ears
beneath a sinister flame,
no pigeon to carry your
words home across the miles
to tell St. Louis
from your own bruised & sobbing cheek
before you were silenced by
unreported hand slid out, hid
& called itself your own, claiming
demise of your nineteen years
your body small inside the sleeves
of tattered uniform,

only screams & litanies
of your wailing sisters,
& ghosts brushing sand
from your eyelids, yearning to
mend your snapped bone
salted vessel singed with lye,
your mother waking into nightmare

your father taking coffin inventory
peels back the glue
under starched gloves concealing,
your smoldered fingers catch his tears
& he nearly drowns in the testimony
of your body, archives
between your skull & the sea
of paper, photographs, evidence, all,
crumbs swept under the service rug,
he hangs on to fight this by his teeth

absurdities in claims, exit wound lies,
assaults washed over you in black & blue
desecration of the brilliance in your eyes

to see your smile once more,
prayers roll out under harsh heart emptiness
full of you, every day full of you

this system is a slaughterhouse housing the weary,
a sty of ruthless invention,
post-traumatic triggers pulling triggers
you were butchered, we know
like a mangled calf shattered cut, we know

somewhere lurking lies a glint truth
choking on threat, we know

the bullet in your head wasn't yours, we know

we know we know we know we know
we know we know we know

helix/womb/house

—(for Basra, for Fallujah)

child, born unmoving in the stillness of an echo,
a gasp bouncing off the roof of your mother's lung,
arriving in twisted arrangement, the bouquet of your limbs, wilted,
injured flowers peddling unsung lullabies to those who can still cry in the
ancient language of conferencing birds,

these imperial feet no longer occupy your weary rooms,
though occupation lingers in the scabbed & pussing wounds,
ground holes, shadows, ghost limbs, dusty photographs of the missing,
chemical downpours shining glossy on your tattered rooftops,
this planted forest of the metal Q swallowed by your scratched eyelids
in the ochre haze of the dawn star shamal morning,
that jaundiced blight stomaching ships at sea & errant roads,
this la'nat dripping from your faucets, swigged before morning prayer,
this cursed deprivation, genocide unleashed & scattering.

child, this is the silver bayonet that pierces the tenanted womb,
the mammoth brute warping
your mother's vast & primal atlas, calling you
to sea before the tide has waned,

child, we have made stones of you unborn, stones & fleshly crooked maps,
cartographies of lost chromosomes, conquered bodies, stolen bricks of time,
we have banished Allah from your epithelial cells,
cast Hajirah to another barren valley,
we have made a house of your dna & placed it under siege, we have
carpet bombed its streets & left your wet heart alone to shrivel in the rubble
of this shattered gallery, helix, womb, home.

what the bird has seen

her eyes the grave
where all the demolitions gone to lie,
where she has buried the certainty of conclusions,
confusions glistening in the sun, fissures
of soil settled over mounds of the unmoving,
the rotted torso deployed to avert subversion,
presiding over unanswered questions, the mineral suite
of implications & excesses, riddled death.

she has seen
the end of sterling sunrises, the harvest
once tempted the fables of generations
out of the mouths of grizzled men
siphoning liquid joy of grapes bursting between the teeth
for tomorrows gifted piecemeal.

she has fathomed the overabundances,
of fish that were never caught, markets
& their dry stalls, vacant shoes, scavenging mothers
praying mothers & mothers unhinged,
the harvest of bones stippling the road, dappling
portaled routes between empty & free, or
between each loneliness under the vacancies
of every kingdom clogging terror into the arterial vestiges
literacies & centuries of teeming heritage,

charred raisins with their gaping rim of lips
composting opera of never again,
brothers, neighbors, hoarded
into a city of the dead, this harrowed
abode without address,
swallowing the dirt of boot soles,
discarded powder of clash tools
built to coerce
the docilities of nations, the mythologies of value,
tenuous & mandated moralities:
day brims chill with the secrets of the silenced.

& this is what the bird has seen,
from the sky, from the spires of holy architectures,
from unshuttered windowsills
the brows of old & daunted trees.

she proffers her testimony, but who can decipher
her warble-whistle, unnerved & quivering,
as it bounces in spurts off these rubbled walls,
into the throng of disoriented ghosts,
bewildered shadows crowding the streets?

like fish, like song

—(mourning for Palestine)

like fish in a waterless barrel, barely breathing;

mosques, crumbling mountains, prayers piled high in the rubble;
the silence of the after;
the limp limb of a dream flattened, cut;

the braided hearts of lovers, thundered from the cord;
the scholar's skull singed barren; a half-polished shoe in a doorway;
tea cup shards & their damp leaves bereft on tomorrow;

lingering smoke steams the mouth, blackens the teeth;

a torn page weeps orphaned paragraphs on the morning's breath,
the melted beauty of trees & their molten archives, the poet's refuge gone;

a cough, an echo, a curse on the sky & the stranger's fist;

the thought that breathing in the dead from an ash-hot wind
is one way to sicken the hunger & thick of dread; is one way to name
the savagery of sorrow, or the sorrow of savagery;

numbness & rage sparring for the aorta, like empty, like lost;

does disbelief catch the tongue;

does a wail make a sound if nobody is left to hear it,
the tympanic membrane housed in the shelled & silent room;

every ear beyond a wall; every question quilted by a silver hair;

every footprint cut short; every knock that left a hole or a shine on the floor;

every secret crevice where hides a God, like hope, like holy, like song up from mud;

like wingless birds in a world that sees a charred nest
& scorches the tree, sets the whole forest ablaze;

in the spring, the Khamsin will carry what remains of the dead,
the dust will settle on our arms, in our rice,
we will brush the dead from our eyes,

we will eat the dead

little birds

they call them paraquitos
reminiscent of little birds,
parakeets, like the ones
your neighbor's abuelita
might keep hanging in a cage
near a window
& cover with a towel at night
for hushing.

yield of paramilitaries
summoning women
unfathomable fathomable,
bullet to husbands fathers clutch,
slitting throats of girls in report
what done to them by whom, these
little children, little paramilitary birds, consequences
in the intervals

left wingless to sleep, swallowed by canyons,
to die of hunger chill hillsides, mothers not want cannot
afraid they devil damned bodies,
impaling bloom broad daylight & terror,
nicked from their nests, stolen seize threat;
mothers remain, spurned by do not see
contamination, social stain, ongoing threat
harrowing days   tarnished agony madness & memory,
            massacre,   unnameable things done,
must, however, be named.

birthed out of vile, burnt in execrable flame
barely a feather to wing their way, charcoal pariahs,
wailing of torment a prefatory lullaby greeting
to this life, throes of nightmare
edge of a mountainside,
furnished with dismemberment
forced traversal of taboos.

birds, little birds
fluttering cage of
near windows unbreakable ache
for home, tenderness of milk & flowers,
little birds, singing their own names in the key of lost,
fluttering, covered at night, interminable night,
with a fist & a gun,
for hushing.

onomasticon (or, I sing the names of our dead)

whenever I sing
there are generations in my throat
reaching out with the long arms
of our old & tattered histories

when I sing, my grief rises like acid
in my throat, cutting my tongue
coating my teeth in red,
       in the fingerprints of a tired hope scratching
       at the broken door, long rusted at the hinges,
       still scratching

I sing, I sing, these fevered words
that fly; these eidetic prophecies:
       a tomorrow once written in the palm,
       lashed in the palm, broken in the palm

I sing the names of our dead & umber, you,
I mount your names on the wall of my mouth,
keep the monument warm,
       & nobody's name will be forgotten
       & nobody's dream will fall unseen, for

when I sing, I sing tree, & bows will sullen bend
with the weight of you, nodding a Morse sorrow

when I sing, I sing pájaro, pájaro, & murmurations burrow the blue,
every wing a messenger, a thunderous feathered conjuring

when I sing, I sing star, & your brilliance lights up my mouth,
illuminates the plains of this weary & bellowing night

I sing rose, & you bloom thorned to scratch your name in the soil,
I sing rise, & the moon climbs over mountains revealing
the road of your arms,

I sing march, & the earth will tremble out a eulogy, a prayer, a promise
I sing how, & why, & when, & your name will wind my palm into a fist, &
I will hold it high

I sing sky, & we will think of freedom, we will taste it,
we will taste it in our mouths, & it will be your name, all your names,
every name of you they think
be gone & done.

the ache on the tongue of the grieving

shatters, splits, tears the mouth in two,
scars the belly beneath the thunder of lead & wailing,

licks the finger, investigating the air near the Line
taste-testing for respite like rain, for night like anguish
battling kehwa down the throat over one lump of sugar for
esophageal wars carrying hostilities to the gut, & the swelling brick
wall rising against the trachea, like a mother's wheezing lament
for the small limp body of her heart, birthed into the dreamless,

bellows in a squirming sleepless nightmare, haunted by
the torment of pliers to the teeth, the swollen eye
peering up slivers of skin plucked by concertina & gripped
by the wall in brittle blood, a neighbor's freckle descried
in the gleam of floodlights, wailing rage gurgling jaw, cut to the gum,

kisses the palms of children before the roof caves in, & knows
the strange accent of the dead indecipherable, though it

echoes against the roof of our frayed & weary mouths.

the value of sparrows

with every daybreak, mourning, sunrise lamentation,
the giving of light shrouded in tempered darkness.

unending night for Fallujah, Basra, others
who have not yet become legible on the map
of congenital disfigurement, traceable trauma, relentless,

distortions of figures staining notions of freedom, dominion
having unhinged the blemish, launched the operations
of demise, poisoned history's present with radiated tears.

these are not monsters, but children, bestowed with the sinister
mirror of collapse malformed, screams mothers censored,
dislocating what was remembered of ages not yet reached,
empire avoiding the insipidity of slow massacres, claiming altruism.

not justice, but its far-reaching veneer, vapors of
the metal Q demons in armor, contrary to diminishment,
even prayers have been annihilated, the syllables of dissimilarity
abolished in disseminations & detriment, piercing skin, bone,
tongue & kin: born are the proverbs of the dispossessed.

a nation sentenced to a future with no future, to disquiet ghosts
that know no borders, & the haunting of anguish has three arms,
or two heads, no skeleton for might. what sort of la'nat have we
unleashed? there will be no answer for generations to come,

or if sooner, in the filament of nightmares tormenting theirs & ours,
contortions of sanity & sense, like the death-bird wandering aimed,
curses of conquest having obliterated families & their tomorrow-roots.

cast to the fringes of lament & burial, how can we ask them to explain
to their children they are not afforded even the value of sparrows?

azan, or
the call to prayer, o
resistir es rezar que arrasemos el orden de arrancamiento, or
when the sky opens & I am swallowed

—(for Aneeta, for Fulan. for N. N.)

> Between 1998 and 2013, over 6,000 undocumented immigrants died
> trying to cross the US-Mexico border.
> —International Organization for Migration,
> Fatal Journeys: Tracking Lives Lost during Migration

> Since 2001, the US has killed over 1.3 million Muslims in its global
> "War on Terror." (This is a conservative estimate.)
> —Physicians for Social Responsibility, Physicians for Global Survival,
> and International Physicians for the Prevention of Nuclear War,
> Body Count: Casualty Figures after Ten Years of the "War on Terror,"
> Iraq, Afghanistan, Pakistan, trans. Ali Fathollah-Nejad

I

on the 6th day,
it rose from dust, this creature we call human,
& there in the folds of our nascent hearts were
ingredients for a ferocious resistance;

we thrashed & gleamed in the giant's eye.

it is written on the wall
that prayer is meaningless unless it is subversive,
& this reminds us that G-d is perhaps nothing but a Question.

II

I have stood in the valley, the pulsing city-heart,
purple dusking into moon-time,
the azan ringing out, echoing down alleyways
as the last cups of kehwa wash down throats
aching to hold the names of Allah
in the temple of the mouth. there, I have seen
the gravedigger's eyes, his mouth full of the names
of every child he was forced to bury, alleged beasts of terror.

Fulan, Fulan,
what was your name?
what was your prayer?

III

I have stood at the edge of the desert, the wide sea
of sun-driven madness, cacti dripping with lost rosaries, hung
like holy, grieving tombstones marking the trail of lost shoes.

N. N.
what did your mother call you?
what saint did you carry around your neck?
who once lost sight of you while tending to laundry,
only to find you again at the table when supper was served?

Natalia Natalia,
the devil lost his poncho:

if you see it, bring it with you,

should you ever return.

till the taste of free in our mouths
(brown baby lullaby)

wake.　　　wake.

these the nights we sing. these the folds,
unborn reverie, ambition marbled mud & shine,
raging anthem born like diamonds out darkest ash & rain
this sky-fist for you, little ones, whose teeth
have yet to bud, whose mouths
will sprout, whose tongues will flower sharpest word,
this fist for you, our future, our want, our tomorrow-yes,

　　　　wake.　　　wake, baby, wake, child.

wake your umber velvet eyelids & cry the sun with us,
these arms around you free
these streets we march, sore grave shaking ground
garnet flooded madness, we mourn
we rake the gravel for teeth so we may have something to bury
we sift the sand for remedy, we ghost-seers carrying our cinnamon dead
we stir the news, history, like an oracle shimmering violent
catching names in our throats before they vanish
under starless storm & urge
we vex the spire, trouble the sway

　　　　wake baby, wake child, this lullaby will break the cage

you will taste the blood of your brothers in our milk, remembering
their glorious beauty as it warms your throat, you will
not know the cold of the concrete that swallowed them whole.
we are a swarm, a pride, a righteous & thick army

wake.   wake.

you will see G-d in the faces of your sisters, you will remember
how they fought five hundred years under an archive of scars, you will
hear their steps when you run, when you
march to the beat of the thundering lung
gasping for air, you will know this fight
to breathe beneath your darkest skin
& you will see & you will raze the reddest fields
gather the pulp of every fruit let it whisper your ear up
sculpt a dream, a name, a vow

till, baby, till, child,

till the taste of free in our mouths

for the boy who went to war & came back fire, came back song

I don't know the names of all the boys who come home,
the fire in their eyes carrying limp babe bodies
whose light gone out, fire like stars want more for the world,
like rusty nails dragging under feet, if feet remain, or one;

fire spit out like yesterday's full metal storms,
running blood & nightmemory askew,
fire like what weighs, swells the heart, smells burning ash in yesterday's nostril,
infects it with the halo of the moon, sign of the unborn & gone;

fire like birth can't undo rain, like rain not wet, like wet don't tear,
like tear burn acidhole in stomach, cheek, the injured moralbone;

fire like song, like guttural wail, railing on the can't no more,
song giving names to little ones on mountaintops
dressed in infinite snowing questions, open fire sustenance song,
fire light world, world cannot hold:
hold you, hold fire, hold your treble, tremble, fire love blazing trail,
fire marrow fighting fear, fireshine, wildfire grave & stone;

I know fire fight, fire mourn, fire scorch the heart, it breathe you in, it burn,
not fail, not under, not too much broken fire mad,
you salty fleshly fire wonder, fire bird & ghost on wing,
I know fire cry, fire sweat up bed sheet,
fire tangle you, rise you up & boom your ear:
you fire, you flame, you radiance,
you star wishing on home, you furnace choir D-string call,
fire fall, voice like yearning thunder, strike, crack me open, fire dark & done;

fire like morning want more for the world, fire out, you, spark remain.

fishbone

the desert devours everything.
even the expectation that it devour everything,
spit nothing out

what does an eight year old alone in the vast greys see
in the mirage rising from earth, rock, gravel,
but his grandmother, the ghost of her,
still alive & weeks away, fresh tamales in hand

how does his mouth, watering for a bit of queso, juice
the baby sister cheek
how does his mouth sweat & pucker for the courage to assure himself
as he assures her in the howling, shadowy night

how dry are his lips that water floods him in nightmares
floods the empty sea of his mouth, naming him Moses
so every desert-walker may safely cross
the border & drink

& drink & drink & drink & drink & drink

the desert devours everything,
even the expectation that it devour everything,
spit nothing out

it devours what it will

spiders weave webs in the skulls of coyotes
a small shoe, flush as the cactus flower
spit out like a fishbone, or
hoisted like a flag, a headstone,
a whole world silent & bright in the dirt.

notes

Introduction

1. Adrienne Rich, *On Lies, Secrets, and Silence: Selected Prose* (New York: W. W. Norton, 1979), 248.

2. Raúl Zurita, "Today or a Million Years Ago: An Interview with Raúl Zurita," by Daniel Borzutzky, in *Harriet* (blog), Poetry Foundation.org, March 24, 2015, https://www.poetryfoundation.org/harriet/2015/03/today-or-a-million-years-ago-an-interview-with-raul-zurita.

To the Poems

LAST BALLOON, epigraph: artist name withheld for protection.

NON-COMBAT RELATED INCIDENTS & OTHER LIES, epigraph: LaVena Johnson is one of many female US military service members deployed to Iraq and Afghanistan whose rape and murders by other US service members have been covered up as suicides by the Department of Defense. See Ann Wright, "US Military Keeping Secrets about Female Soldiers' 'Suicides'?" Common Dreams, August 31, 2008, https://www.commondreams.org/views/2008/08/31/us-military-keeping-secrets-about-female-soldiers-suicides.

HELIX/WOMB/HOUSE: Depleted Uranium (DU), otherwise known as Q-metal, depleted alloy, or D-38, is a radioactive heavy metal with proven genotoxicity. DU munitions used and dumped in Iraq by the US and UK militaries have been connected to the sharp increase in stillbirths, miscarriages, congenital birth defects, and cancer rates reported in Iraq since 2001. The United States and its major stakeholders continue to deny any correlation between the two issues and have not taken action to clean up the contamination. The failure of the United States to assume responsibility for this radioactive and chemically toxic metal, and its impact on the reproductive health of the Iraqi people, must be viewed as a form of social cleansing—a pernicious effect of US militarization and its attendant human rights abuses. For more information, see the report by IKV Pax Christi, *In a State of Uncertainty: Impact and Implications of the Use of Depleted Uranium in Iraq*, January 2013, http://www.bandepleteduranium.org/en/docs/205.pdf.

THE ACHE ON THE TONGUE OF THE GRIEVING: The poem title is inspired by Laurie Ann Guerrero's book title *A Tongue in the Mouth of the Dying*.

HEIDI ANDREA RESTREPO RHODES
is a queer, mixed-race, latinx second-generation Colombian
immigrant, poet, artist, scholar, and activist. A 2018 Voices of Our
Nation Arts (VONA) alum, her poetry has been published in *As/Us*,
[Pank], *Raspa*, *Word Riot*, *Feminist Studies*, *Huizache*, and *Write
Bloody*, among other places. Born in Arizona and raised in California,
she currently lives in Brooklyn.

CPSIA information can be obtained
at www.ICGtesting.com
Printed in the USA
LVHW081815150319
610815LV00014B/579/P